Wildflowers
of the Rock

Dennis Minty

BREAKWATER

BREAKWATER
100 Water Street
P.O. Box 2188
St. John's, NF
Canada, A1C 6E6

The Publisher gratefully acknowledges the financial assistance of the Canada Council which has helped make this publication possible.

The Publisher acknowledges the financial assistance of the Cultural Affairs Division, Department of Municipal and Provincial Affairs, Government of Newfoundland and Labrador which has made this publication possible.

Canadian Cataloguing in Publication Data
   Minty, Dennis.

      Wildflowers of the rock

      ISBN 1-55081-103-7

   1. Wild flowers — Newfoundland — Pictorial works.
   2. Berries — Newfoundland — Pictorial works.
   I. Title.

   QK203.N4M56 1995   582.13'09718   C95-950133-9

Printed and bound in Hong Kong.

Acknowledgements

I would like to thank Clyde Rose for the idea to do this book and for his continuing enthusiasm, Dr. Peter Scott for reviewing the text for botanical accuracy and confirming identifications, Dr. Alexander (Sandy) Robertson also for his botanical wisdom, Nadine Osmond for the design and layout, and Laura Woodford for her careful editorial eye. I would also like to thank the various authors who kindly granted permission to reprint their poems throughout this book.

Preface

This is an intimate exploration of some of Newfoundland's wildflowers and berries. Interpretive, rather than documentary, it attempts to reveal their beauty against a spartan, often severe, environmental backdrop. This book is not intended as a scholarly and comprehensive botanical treatment. The focus is on beauty and setting, rather than scientific information. These plants do not grow randomly about the landscape; each is fine-tuned for its own place in the world. My hope is that you will see these gentle beauties as essential ingredients of nature, no more or less important than any other life. After all, it is one world, and we are but a part.

Introduction

About 10,000 years ago, most of this place was scoured clean by glaciers that left behind either barren, cold rock or gravelly debris. Today's soil, a pathetic skim in most places, has developed since the ice sheets disappeared. As if this isn't a meagre enough basis for growth, the Labrador Current throws a cold shroud over the land at its edge and the wind dares anything to grow at all. These are the predominant influences on the floral composition of this place. If flowers were an athletic team, the 'Wildflowers of the Rock' would be underdogs with daunting stamina that would make a coach proud.

Aster

Aster puniceus

At woodland edges and stream borders, the low, morning light of fall reveals frosted asters often wreathed with webs. Together with their usual neighbour, goldenrod, these are among the most notable flowers of fall. There are fourteen species of asters in Newfoundland much to the gratification of many small birds that favour their seeds. The one shown here is the purple-stemmed aster.

Bladderwort

Utricularia cornuta

This orchid-like little flower emerges from bog pools from June to August. Its submerged foliage has small bladders surrounded at their entrance by bristly sensors. A wayward insect touching the sensors triggers the trap which suddenly sucks in a gush of water, complete with insect, into the bladder. The little bug then dies and its bodily goodness is absorbed by the plant. As with the pitcher-plant and the sundew, this is an adaptation that helps the horned bladderwort survive in a nutrient-poor environment.

Marsh

sun on whorl
  of pitcher plant
  and finger tip

scattered raindrops
  your fistful of berries
  pattering on tin

  mist on my face
white light
through wing of dragonfly

  heat ripples
moth dance
over beaver sticks

         — Tom Dawe

Blue Flag

Iris versicolor

Iris, the goddess of the rainbow is no doubt pleased to have this decadent blossom named after her; but little did she know that a poison—iridin, lurks in its stem. This wild iris likes very wet and rich ground where it blooms from July to early August. In spite of its poisonous content, some native peoples have used it to alleviate colds and lung problems, and in poultices to ease burns or boils. This is my daughter Sarah's favourite flower, so much so that her mother crafted for her a graduation dress with a bodice of silk irises and a tail reminiscent of verdant, swaying leaves.

Bluebell *(Harebell)*

Campanula rotundifolia

For such a delicate flower, this token of the fairy-world chooses ridiculously harsh places to live. All summer long, bluebells, or harebells, bloom on windblown, rocky headlands or along the edges of exposed, coastal greens. The Latin name means little bell with round leaves. If they were bells, they would create the most delightful music since, in every breath of wind, they totter on stalks not much stouter than a few hairs. Bluebells tease my camera constantly, calling to be snapped, but rarely cooperating as they dance to the 'rock' music.

> *The harebell had always from a child been with me a favourite flower;....*

— Susanna Moodie, 1852

Abandoned Outport

Sun on boarded windows
and gull cries
high in August clouds.

On a small beach-path:
blue-bells nodding
over driftwood.

A bee is buzzing
inside dark cracks
in a window pane.

Clover meadow:
above the rusting ploughshare
a butterfly.

A sudden fog
and sea-winds
bend the sting-nettle.

Deep in graveyard grass
snails and lichens
cling to the headstone.

Across the schoolhouse floor:
paper scraps, dry sea-weed
and a dead moth.

Against the cold twilight:
dark picket-fences
and a crow's flight.

In a rising moon:
a church steeple
and lilac leaves.

— *Tom Dawe*

Blueberry

Vaccinium angustifolium

When the blueberry leaves turn flame-red in the fall, I want to be on the barrens. For picker and partridge, these juicy globes are the stuff of life and without them the barrens would be barren indeed. My mother lived for their ripening in August and, with iron stove bedecked with pots, she transformed them into the finest of hot pies and sumptuous, dark jams. Although they can make a fine red wine, my family never quite made the grade. Nonetheless, in jar and cask, berries, water and sugar were combined each year. Round about Christmas, we might have the occasional eruption cloaking the kitchen walls and ceiling with the sweet, fermented beverage. Picking the skins out of the butter and sugar was an engaging pastime.

Bogbean

Menyanthes trifoliata

From a few paces away this looks like a humble little white blossom, but up close its intricate form is captivating. From June to July it flowers in shallow water pools. Buckbean, bog myrtle, water shamrock and bog hop are alternate names used in other places. The last one no doubt comes from the practice, in times past, of using its roots to flavour beer. The dried foliage has also been made into a hot infusion and used as a tonic.

Bottlebrush

Sanguisorba canadensis

Having spent many hours washing milk bottles with an identical looking device, I prefer the descriptive local name, bottlebrush, to the perhaps more common Canadian burnet. It grows in poorly drained areas and blooms from July to October. The burnets have been much favoured by herbalists for decades, both because of the cucumber-like flavour of the leaves and because of their medicinal qualities. It is said that the Tudors of England used burnets to cure gout and rheumatism.

> *The leaves stiped in wine and dronken, doth comfort*
> *and rejoice the hart, and are good against trembling*
> *and shaking of the same.*

— Dodoens, date unknown

Buttercup

Ranunculus spp.

I always wondered why as children we tested our fondness for butter by holding a buttercup close under the chin and looking for a golden cast; I knew I liked it with or without buttercup radiance on my chin. There are more than thirty species of buttercups that grow in eastern North America. They bloom from late June to August in meadows and pastures. In my father's pastures although all the grass was close-cropped from the cow's grazing, they would always leave the buttercups. They contain a juice—bitter when fresh, but bland when dry.

Haiku (1)

dawn flecks
in lees
of buttercup

doryman
lifts herring-net
and morning moon

— Tom Dawe

Corn-lily

Clintonia borealis

Most Newfoundland children will tell you: "Those are poison berries!" Although the berries are not considered edible, their young leaves taste like cucumber and are good raw in salads or boiled as greens. Also known as the blue-bead lily in some places, its home is in mixed woodlands where the flaring, corn-coloured bloom appears in June.

Cotton Grass

Eriophorum sp.

On the side of Saglek Fjord, with the Torngat Mountains of
northern Labrador stretching to the north, I found what looked
like the root-source of all the world's cotton grass—a veritable
breeding colony. Like a frosted, floating meadowland, they
swayed with each waft of mountain air across the inlet. This
sedge is also known as Hare's Tails and 'puffs out' in late May
or early June on many peatlands throughout the province.
I wonder if they all started from here on Saglek Fjord?

Crackerberry

Cornus canadensis

Around early July, the forest floor brightens with the white
blossoms of this member of the dogwood family. Then, in late
summer, the scarlet fruit, also known as bunchberries, invite the
hands of small children to try a taste. The tight-skinned berries
'crack' as young teeth burst through, but the taste is disappointing
to most. Nonetheless, they are nutritious and many birds, mice
and squirrels find them quite acceptable—so did my toddling
son, Adam.

Dandelion

Taraxacum officinale

The jagged leaf gave rise to the French name 'dente de lion', or in English, lion's tooth. In this area, they don't hold quite the same level of respect and are known as 'piss-a-beds'. In spite of the lowly reputation of this beleaguered flower in the eyes of lawn manicurists, it is not all bad. It is often listed in books on herbal medicine as a diuretic, laxative or tonic. The flowers make a delicate golden wine and the rest of the plant is traditionally eaten as greens.

> *Its root is sold at St. John's, in spring, by children who gather it in the gardens and fields, and in the absence of other fresh vegetables, after a long winter, it is much relished....*

> — Sir Richard Henry Bonnycastle, Newfoundland, 1842

Song for Dandelion

Because it mirrors the sun.
Because it cheers waste spaces.
Because it ignores orders.
Because it is a wanderer.
Because it sings in this acid soil.
Because its roots are coffee.
Because its flowers are wine.
Because its seeds are a circle of mist.
Because it puns.
Because it has lions' teeth.
Because it is invincible.

— Mary Dalton

Dogberry

Sorbus americana

One of my favourite trees in Newfoundland sits in a tiny cove
along the north arm of Trinity Harbour. With few onlookers, it
puts on a show each fall as its leaves yellow as a poignant backdrop for its brilliant berries. Those who come up with the clever
names for colours should use 'dogberry' as the standard for
orange-red. It is one of nature's shouts to pay attention! In other
places, it is known as American dogberry or mountain ash. The
berries persist throughout the winter and draw birds as bland
as starlings and as debonair as waxwings. My Aunt Marion was
drawn to them too, and made one of the earth's finest, tart jellies
that ever graced a piece of warm, crunchy toast.

Everlasting Daisy *(Pearly Everlasting)*

Anaphalis margaritacea

My mother gathered these delicate blooms during a fall trek around the farm most every year. They grew in dry soils along the pasture edges. She would tie them together in small bunches and hang them over the kitchen stove to dry. While drying, the blossoms would usually open a bit more, showing their yellow centres. She would assemble them into a bouquet, perhaps with wild rose hips, that would grace our dining room table the winter long. Whenever I see them, I think of my mother's hands—an everlasting memory.

Goldenrod

Solidago spp.

The first frosts of fall often catch these golden fronds in full bloom. With wild asters, which are usually nearby, they remind fall that it takes more than a few frosty mornings to put summer to bed. Goldenrod springs up along roadside ditches, the edges of fields or other recently disturbed or exposed areas, denouncing the comforts of rich till. Although physically much different, it is a member of the sunflower family—appropriately so, since its intense yellow should lift any viewer above dull thoughts.

Indian Pipe

Monotropa uniflora

This odd plant likes the stillness and shade of the deep woods, arising out of the duff of the forest floor at the peak of summer. I suppose it earns its alternate name, corpse-plant, from its ghostly appearance, like the translucent skin of the dead. This, combined with the fact that it lives off decaying organic matter, makes it easy to imagine supernatural qualities associated with this delicate member of the wintergreen family.

Juniper

Juniperus communis

Based on the 1865 survey by J.H. Kerr, the navigational chart for the eastern part of Trinity Bay shows a landmark named Ginpickers Hill towards the eastern end of Random Island. No doubt ground juniper grows there in abundance because it is these cloudy-blue berries that are used to flavour gin. This evergreen flourishes in dry woods and rocky hillsides, in gravelly, well-drained soil. Whenever one of my father's cows was about to have a calf, I would be sent to fetch an armful of ground juniper which would be steeped out in a large boiler on the kitchen stove. The rich, piney aroma filled the house and made me think of stimulants for growing hair on bald heads. After cooling a bit, this broth would be given to the cow soon after the calf was delivered. She would down the vitamin-rich tonic as though it was the first liquid to be seen after a long desert crossing. The berries also make a fine garnish when cooked with game or poultry, reducing the gamey taste of some meats.

Labrador Tea

Ledum groenlandicum

This member of the heath family is easily recognized by its leathery leaf with rolled edge and rust-coloured fuzz on its underside. The young leaves and twigs are eaten by moose, caribou and ptarmigan. You can pick and dry the leaves and make them into a tea, but the tea should not be allowed to boil because it can then release harmful chemicals. Also known as Indian tea, it flowers from June to August on bogs, barrens and poorly drained areas.

> *Since our departure from Point Lake we had boiled the Indian tea plant…which produced a beverage in smell much resembling rhubarb; notwithstanding which we found it refreshing, and were gratified to see this plant flourishing abundantly, though of dwarfish growth, on the sea-shore.*

> — Sir John Franklin, 1823

Ox-eye Daisy

Chrysanthemum leucanthemum

This is one of the most common flowers alongside roads and in meadows and pastures. A member of the sunflower family, it was probably introduced from Europe but now it is naturalized. Like the buttercup, it is not liked by dairy farmers because of the unpleasant taste it can impart to milk.

Microcosm

*Lying in a meadow
mint-scented, brook-lulled,
you're looking up now
into star-thronged heavens
with your lover beside you
in the warm sleeping bag:
your pulse returns to normal
and you can almost feel
the tranquil constellations
revolving, far within
the heart's veined ruby.*

— Neil Murray

Partridgeberry

Vaccinium vitis-idaea

In Labrador this is the redberry, in the Maritimes, foxberry and in some other places, mountain cranberry. In Newfoundland it is the queen of the wild berries, staking claim to barren, rocky hillsides. Its tiny pink blossoms are out from mid-June to mid-July and the berries ripen around mid-September. Ptarmigan and caribou eat these berries through fall and winter and some long-distance, migratory birds use them to refuel before setting off across the water to places more benign. Those of us who stay, feast through the winter on tart pies, piquant jams bumpily spread on fresh bread, and ice-cream topping to kill for.

Pitcher-plant

Sarracenia purpurea

The beautifully sinister pitchers of this bog-dweller lure insects with their bright colour and pungent smell. Once inside the lip of one, the insects are doomed. Downward-pointing hairs prevent their upward climb and eventually they tumble into the pool of digestive juices at the bottom and drown. The plant then absorbs their goodness and is thereby able to thrive in nutrient-poor peat bogs. But some organisms are so specialized that they have chosen the murky juice in the pitcher as their home. One kind of mosquito spends its larval period swimming and feeding in this liquid comfort. This unusual, carnivorous plant is the floral emblem of Newfoundland and Labrador.

> *But of all the natural productions of the swamps none is more singular than the water-bearer, pitcher-plant,....*

— Sir Richard Henry Bonnycastle, Newfoundland, 1842

On Small Island

on path moss
    up from landwash
leaf sounds

in from sea
    cat paws
through long grass

bisecting pool
    and sky
the muskrat's wake

raindrops
    rock reflections
in lily pads

from grass spear
    sun drops
into pitcher plant

       — Tom Dawe

Rhodora

Rhododendron canadense

Like the March hare muttering "I'm late, I'm late…" this flower seems to be in a hurry. It blooms in June before most other plants and even before its own leaves develop. The gorgeous blossoms enlighten spring walks that might take you near the margins of bogs, barrens or poorly-drained areas.

Roseroot

Sedum rosea

Along the shores of the volcanic islands of Notre Dame Bay, roseroot is common. Like the people of this place, it stubbornly anchors to fissures in the craggy rock and ekes out a living in these most rigorous conditions. It flowers from June to July; males are yellow and females are reddish-brown.

Sand Piper

It hopped
across the pool-streaked sand
as the tide was coming in,
with legs like straws
that would not bend,
and a low, piping call
on the rising wind.

It skipped
along the mussel-beds
as the sun dropped
from the sky,
and faded somewhere
in the surf
with a lonely, twittering cry.

— Tom Dawe

Round-leaved Sundew

Drosera rotundifolia

Smaller than the tip of your finger, the leaves of this delicate plant are in the same lethal league as the pitcher-plant. The sticky droplets at the end of each red spike lure and trap small insects and spiders. Then, like a hand closing on a morsel of candy, the leaf closes upon the bug and digests it. The sticky droplets form only after it opens again so the leaf doesn't glue itself shut. By using the little insect to supplement its diet, it is perfectly suited for the nutrient-poor bog environment. Never having noticed it before, you may think this is a rare plant—not so. Anyone who has walked across a bog has placed a foot very near or on top of this glistening jewel.

Sheep Laurel

Kalmia angustifolia

This vigorous member of the heath family can be found in many different habitats such as bogs, barrens, old pastures and woodlands. It is called by many names such as lambkill, goo-witty, gold-withy, and several other minor variations of these. Children in Twillingate refer to the bright pink flowers that bloom from late June to early August, as cups and saucers. As the name lambkill suggests, this plant is poisonous to livestock, but some wild animals such as snowshoe hare don't seem to mind it.

Water-lily

Nymphaea odorata, Nuphar variegata

You can slip from adoration to vexation in a few seconds if a mud trout on the end of your fishing line chooses to seek refuge amongst the stout stems of these beauties. You can commonly encounter two kinds of water-lilies in this province—the yellow bullhead-lily and the white, fragrant water-lily. All grow in quiet, shallow ponds and flower from June to September, their blossoms opening in the morning and closing in the afternoon. Some refer to them as beaver root because beavers (as well as muskrats and moose) relish the stems and roots. Their young leaves, unopened buds and roots are edible. In some cultures they are considered symbols of perfection because of the way the flowers float, seemingly untouched by muddy water.

> *...we glided through vast fields of white water-lilies; it was perpetual variety, perpetual beauty, perpetual delight and enchantment,....*

> — Anna Brownwell Jameson, 1838

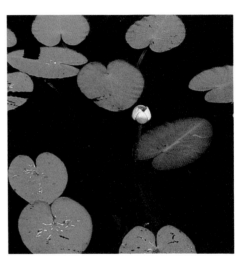

Wild Rose

Rosa nitida and *Rosa rugosa*

Also known as the northeastern rose (*R. nitida*), this is a member of one of the world's most beautiful and useful plant families. Its value has been recognized for millennia. Ancient Persians favoured them in their gardens and rose petals have been found in Egyptian tombs. The wild rose of this province, a more humble version with its simple flower and relatively small hip or fruit, grows in poorly drained areas, around bogs and fens, and alongside brooks. The rough rose (*R. rugosa*), known for its abundance of large, succulent hips, is an imported species now growing wild especially in a number of abandoned settlements around the coast. Rose hips are greatly valued by herbalists who claim that, gram for gram, hips contain forty to sixty times more Vitamin C than oranges. I have read that during the wartime of the 1940s many children in Britain and Scandinavia may not have survived were it not for their consumption of wholesome, wild rose hips. I can testify that a hot, buttered tea bun topped with a dollop of fragrant, rose hip jelly is worth stopping for.

Wild Strawberry

Fragaria virginiana

Thousands of diminutive strawberry plants grow amongst
the thick grass on the eastern headland of Crocker's Cove,
Conception Bay, and in similar spots all over Newfoundland.
They flower early in May or June and produce their tasty little
berries in July and August. They make a delicious jam if you
have the patience to pick enough, but if you don't, you can
use a dozen or so to make a fragrant tea. For me, a single berry
savoured in a warm, salty breeze can symbolize the best
of Newfoundland summer.

Song Also

a reply to Pat Lowther

Take me to your island.
I'll speak so softly
you'll have to feel my words
whispering on your skin.
Coming from my own island
I know very well how sound
carries across water.
I'll come in the blackest night
of the year and walk with you
through the twisted trees
to the sea.
And we'll collect
whatever jewelled creatures
you want to wish up
out of the onyx ocean.
We'll lie side by side on the sand
and let the sky touch us
where it will.
I'll wear my warmest skin
and follow wherever you go.
And I'll speak only silence
if you'll take me.

— Al Pittman